Little Prayers to Mary

- Holy Mary, pray for us.

- Sweet heart of Mary,
  be my salvation.

- Holy Mary, make my heart
  and my soul pure.

- Mother of love,
  pray for us.

- O Mary conceived without
  sin, pray for us who have
  recourse to you.

- Queen of heaven,
  pray for us to God.

This book belongs to

Date ------------------------------

Presented by

My First
PRAYERBOOK

By REV. LAWRENCE G. LOVASIK, S.V.D.
Divine Word Missionary

NIHIL OBSTAT: James T. O'Connor, S.T.D., Censor Librorum
IMPRIMATUR: Patrick J. Sheridan, Vicar General, Archdiocese of New York

The Nihil Obstat and Imprimatur are official declarations that a book or pamphlet is free of doctrinal or moral error. No implication is contained therein that those who have granted the Nihil Obstat and Imprimatur agree with the contents, opinions or statements expressed.

Printed in Hong Kong   ISBN 978-0-89942-205-3

TALKING TO GOD

When we pray, we raise our hearts and minds to God. We talk to God: Father, Son, and Holy Spirit. We adore God as our Creator. We give Him thanks for all His blessings. We beg His forgiveness for our faults. We ask for His help in our daily lives. We can also pray to Mary the Mother of Jesus and to the Saints who had great love for Jesus. They will ask God to help us.

The Glory Be

Glory be to the Father,
and to the Son,
and to the Holy Spirit.

As it was in the beginning,
is now, and ever shall be,
world without end. Amen.

We must give thanks to God as long as we live. We give thanks to the Heavenly Father for sending His Son to redeem us and for sending the Holy Spirit to make us holy.

MORNING PRAYER

Thank You, O God,
for this new day.

Help me in body and soul,
in my work and play.

Bless all I do or think or say.

Let me do everything to please You,
and keep me from all danger and sin.

PRAYER DURING THE DAY

Jesus, You are the joy of my heart.
Even though I do not see You,
I know that You are with me
   if I stay in Your grace and love You.

Help me to think of You often during the day,
   even when I am playing.
I want to tell You often
   that I love You very much.

God has given us our parents to watch over us and teach us about Him. We should pray for them every day.

PRAYER FOR OUR FAMILY

Dear Jesus, I beg You
    to give Your special graces to our family.
May our home be a place of peace,
    holiness, and love.
Protect us from all sin
    and keep us close to Your Heart.

Mary, loving Mother of Jesus and our Mother,
    pray to Jesus for our family.
Keep us in Your loving care.

Good Saint Joseph,
    help us in all our needs.
Watch over our home and keep us safe.

Dear God, Father, Son and Holy Spirit,
    we thank You for Your goodness to us.
Give us Your grace
    to love and serve You on earth
    so that we may be worthy
    to be with You in heaven.

PRAYER FOR MY TEACHERS

L ord, my teachers work hard
    to help me learn
        many important things I have to know
        in my daily life.

Thank You for my teachers,
    and all who teach me about You.

Help me to study hard
    to please them and especially You.

PRAYER FOR MY PRIESTS

Dear Lord,
bless our Holy Father,
our bishops and priests,
who take Your place among us.

They teach us Your truth,
take away our sins,
and offer Holy Mass.

Bless all those who teach us
to know and love You.
Reward them in heaven.

God has given us friends who play with us and make our lives happier. We should pray for our friends every day.

PRAYER FOR MY FRIENDS

Jesus, You love children.
When their mothers brought them,
You laid Your hands on them in prayer
and blessed them.
You said, "Let the children come to Me.
The Kingdom of God belongs to such as these."

You were once a Child like me
and had friends to play with You.
Bless me and all the friends You gave me.

Help us to be kind to each other
as You always were.

When I work or study or play with my friends,
may I always be good to them.

Keep us from all that is bad
that we may all be Your friends.
Give us Your grace
through prayer and Holy Communion
that our souls may be beautiful
and pleasing to our Heavenly Father.

PRAYER AT TABLE

Prayer before Meals

Bless us, O Lord,
and these Your gifts,
which we are about to receive
from Your goodness,
through Christ our Lord. Amen.

Prayer after Meals

We thank You, O God,
for all these gifts,
which we have received from Your goodness,
through Christ our Lord. Amen.

Each day God provides food for us to eat so that we may remain healthy and grow. We should thank God every time we sit down at table.

EVENING PRAYER

O God, I thank You
for being good to me.

Forgive me for anything I have done
to displease You this day.
I am sorry!

Bless my father and mother,
my brothers and sisters,
all those I love,
and the children of the whole world.

PRAYER BEFORE CONFESSION

O my God,
   I am heartily sorry
for having offended You,
and I detest all my sins,
because of Your just punishments,
but most of all,
because they offend You, my God,
Who are all-good
and deserving of all my love.

I firmly resolve,
   with the help of Your grace,
to sin no more
and to avoid the near occasions of sin.
Amen.

At Mass God gives us the Body and Blood of Jesus as spiritual food and drink. We should thank Jesus for coming to us and ask for His help.

16

PRAYER AT MASS

Jesus, I believe that at the Last Supper,
You gave us the Holy Eucharist—
the sacrifice of Your Body and Blood—
to continue for all time
the sacrifice of the Cross.

You gave Your Church this remembrance
of Your death and resurrection.

The priest at Mass,
by the power he receives from You,
really brings You on the altar
and offers You to God the Father,
in the name of all the people.

I join my prayers with Yours at Mass
and offer You to Your Father in heaven,
to adore Him as my God and Father,
to thank Him for all He has done for me,
to ask His pardon for my sins,
and to beg Him to give me all I need.

God created this wonderful world to show His love for us. We should remember to thank Him from time to time.

PRAYER TO
OUR HEAVENLY FATHER

Heavenly Father, I thank You
for the life You gave me
and for all the things You do
to make me happy in this world.

I thank You for the stars and sky,
for the hills and fields and lakes,
for flowers, trees, and grass,
for birds and all the animals.

You made all these things.

Never let me forget
Your love for me.

I give You all my love
and all that I do.

I want to be good to please You
as Your loving child.

Thank You, my dearest God,
for being my Father.

Jesus Christ became man, like one of us, that He might teach us, die on the Cross for us, rise from the dead, and be our King.

PRAYER TO JESUS
OUR KING

Jesus, You came on earth
   to be our King
   and our Best Friend.

You teach us how to live
   in order to please You and the Father.

Help me to be close to You,
   to avoid sin and do good.

Keep me ever in Your grace
   and in close union with You.

I want to make You my Best Friend
   for my whole life.

My Lord and my God,
   I love You with my whole heart.

PRAYER TO THE HOLY SPIRIT

Holy Spirit, my God,
the Third Person
of the Blessed Trinity,
I love You.

You are the Love of God
the Father and the Son.

They sent You to the Church
to make it holy.

I thank You for the grace
You have given me
to make my soul beautiful
and to help me to be good.

Your grace made me a child of God;
it opened heaven to me.

Holy Spirit, live in my soul,
and take me to heaven someday.

The Holy Spirit is pictured as a dove and the rays are the graces He pours out into our hearts. We should thank Him for the great helps He lovingly gives us.

Mary, the Mother of Jesus, is also our Mother. She loves and prays for us before God in heaven. We should pray to her every day by using the words of the "Hail Mary."

PRAYER TO MARY OUR MOTHER

Blessed Virgin Mary,
 Jesus gave you to me
 as my Mother
 when He was dying on the Cross.

I want to love you as Jesus did.

I pray to you in these words:

The Hail Mary

Hail Mary, full of grace!
 The Lord is with thee;
 blessed art thou among women,
 and blessed is the fruit
 of thy womb, Jesus.

Holy Mary, Mother of God,
 pray for us sinners,
 now and at the hour
 of our death. Amen.

PRAYER TO MY PATRON SAINT

Dear Saint N.,
   I have been honored to bear your name,
   which you made famous by your holiness.
Help me never to shame this name.

Obtain God's grace for me
   that I may grow in faith, hope, and love,
   and all the virtues.

Grant that by imitating you I may imitate
   your Lord and Master, Jesus Christ.

Watch over me all my life
   and bring me safe to my heavenly home.

PRAYER TO
MY GUARDIAN ANGEL

Angel of God
my Guardian dear,
God's love for me
has sent you here.

Ever this day
be at my side,
to light and guard,
to rule and guide.

My dear Guardian Angel,
teach me to know God,
to love and serve Him
and save my soul.

Keep me from all danger,
and lead me to heaven.

THE ROSARY

The Rosary is a devotional prayer honoring the Mother of God. It is said on a string of beads made up of five sets each of one large and ten smaller beads, called decades. On the large beads the Our Father is said; on the small ones, the Hail Mary.

While saying twenty decades, we think about the joyous, luminous, sorrowful, or glorious parts of Our Lord and Our Lady's life, called the Mysteries of the Rosary.

At Lourdes, France, in 1858, the Blessed Virgin appeared to Bernadette and said the Rosary with her. At Fatima, Portugal, in 1917, she said the Rosary with the three children to whom she appeared, and said, "I am the Lady of the Rosary, and I have come to warn the faithful to amend their lives and ask pardon for their sins. People must not continue to offend the Lord Who is already so deeply offended. They must say the Rosary."

The Rosary is a Sacramental. The Rosary is a devotion most pleasing to our Blessed Mother and to Our Lord, because during the recitation of the Our Father and Hail Mary we think about their lives and the love they showed for us.

THE MYSTERIES OF THE HOLY ROSARY

THE JOYFUL MYSTERIES

1. The Annunciation
2. The Visitation
3. The Nativity
4. The Presentation in the Temple
5. The Finding of the Child Jesus in the Temple

THE LUMINOUS MYSTERIES

1. The Baptism of Jesus
2. The Wedding Feast at Cana
3. The Proclamation of the Kingdom
4. The Transfiguration
5. The Institution of the Eucharist

THE SORROWFUL MYSTERIES

1. The Agony in the Garden
2. The Scourging
3. The Crowning with Thorns
4. The Carrying of the Cross
5. The Crucifixion

THE GLORIOUS MYSTERIES

1. The Resurrection
2. The Ascension
3. The Descent of the Holy Spirit
4. The Assumption
5. The Coronation of the Blessed Virgin

29

PRAYER FOR MY PETS

Jesus, I thank You for the many things
You give me that make my life happy.

You give me the little animals
to be my companions.

They remind me
of how much You care for me.

I want to be kind to my pets
and to all animals
because You made them to give You glory.

PRAYER ON MY BIRTHDAY

Dear Jesus, I thank You
for each day of my life.

It is a gift from You.

Help me to use it well
to serve You and the people
I meet each day.

Thank You for each birthday
that makes me think of Your love for me.

When my life on earth is over,
take me to heaven
to live with You forever.

31

THE PRAYER OF JESUS

"**O**ur Father, Who art in heaven,
hallowed be Thy Name.
The Kingdom come.
Thy will be done on earth
as it is in heaven.
Give us this day our daily bread;
and forgive us our trespasses
as we forgive those who trespass against us.
And lead us not into temptation,
but deliver us from evil."

Other Great Books for Children

FIRST MASS BOOK—Ideal Children's Mass Book with all the official Mass prayers. Colored illustrations of the Mass and the Life of Christ. Confession and Communion Prayers.   Ask for No. 808

The STORY OF JESUS—By Father Lovasik, S.V.D. A large-format book with magnificent full colored pictures for young readers to enjoy and learn about the life of Jesus. Each story is told in simple and direct words.   Ask for No. 535

CATHOLIC PICTURE BIBLE—By Rev. L. Lovasik, S.V.D. Thrilling, inspiring and educational for all ages. Over 110 Bible stories retold in simple words, and illustrated in full color.   Ask for No. 435

LIVES OF THE SAINTS—New Revised Edition. Short life of a Saint and prayer for every day of the year. Over 50 illustrations. Ideal for daily meditation and private study.   Ask for No. 870

PICTURE BOOK OF SAINTS—By Rev. L. Lovasik, S.V.D. Illustrated lives of the Saints in full color. It clearly depicts the lives of over 100 popular Saints in word and picture.   Ask for No. 235

Saint Joseph CHILDREN'S MISSAL—This new beautiful Children's Missal, illustrated throughout in full color. Includes official Responses by the people. An Ideal gift for First Holy Communion.
Ask for No. 806

St. Joseph FIRST CHILDREN'S BIBLE—By Father Lovasik, S.V.D. Over 50 of the best-loved stories of the Bible retold for children. Each story is written in clear and simple language and illustrated by an attractive and superbly inspiring illustration. A perfect book for introducing very young children to the Bible.   Ask for No. 135

WHEREVER CATHOLIC BOOKS ARE SOLD

Index of Prayers